World at Risk

FEEDING THE WORLD

Anne Rooney

A+

Smart Apple Media

Smart Apple Media
P.O. Box 3263
Mankato, MN 56002

Printed in the United States of America

Library of Congress Cataloging-in-Publication Data

Rooney, Anne.
  Feeding the world / by Anne Rooney.
    p. cm. -- (World at risk)
  Includes index.
  ISBN 978-1-59920-377-5 (hardcover)
  1. Food supply--Juvenile literature. 2. Conservation of natural resources--Juvenile literature. 3. Environmental protection--Juvenile literature. I. Title.
  HD9000.5.R63 2010
  363.8--dc22

                                                                                                    2009005975

Created by Q2AMedia
Editor: Penny Dowdy
Art Director: Rahul Dhiman
Designer: Harleen Mehta
Picture Researcher: Shreya Sharma

All words in **bold** can be found in the glossary on pages 42–43.

Web site information is correct at time of going to press. However, the publishers cannot
accept liability for any information or links found on third-party web sites.

Picture credits
t=top b=bottom c=center l=left r=right

Cover Images: Shutterstock: bg, Inset: Hanna Mariah: cl Lucian Coman/Shutterstock: c, Robert Adrian Hillman/Shutterstock: cr.

Insides: Pomortzeff/Dreamstime: Title Page, Martin Chalou/Shutterstock: content Page, Shadow/Shutterstock: 9, Tony Wear/Shutterstock: 10, Eduardo Verdugo/Associated Press: 11, David Noton Photography/Alamy: 12, Matt Apps/Shutterstock: 13, Peter Turnley/Corbis:14, Hemis/Alamy: 16, Peter Turnley/Corbis: 17, Bettmann/Corbis: 18, Joseph Luoman /iStockphoto: 19, Photo Create/Shutterstock: 20, Janeb/Bigstockphoto: 21, Ersler Dmitry/Shutterstock: 22, Galyna Andrushko/Shutterstock: 23, Nigel Cattlin/Alamy: 24, Adrian Hillman/ iStockphoto: 25, Archivo Museo Salesiano/ De Agostini, Greenpeace/Daniel Beltra: 26, Robert Adrian Hillman/ Shutterstock: 27, Sean Sprague/Alamy: 28, Shao Weiwei/Shutterstock: 29, Vera Bogaerts/Shutterstock: 30, Sandra Cunningham/ Shutterstock: 31, Lynsey Allan/ Shutterstock: 32, Ritu Raj Konwar/The Hindu: 33, Christophe Ena/ Associated Press: 34, Pomortzeff/ Dreamstime: 35, Dita Alangkar/ Associated Press: 36, R Shivaji Rao/The Hindu: 37, John Lindsay-Smith/ Shutterstock: 38, Images&Stories/Alamy: 39.

Q2AMedia Art Bank: 8, 15, 40, 41.

9 8 7 6 5 4 3 2 1

CONTENTS

1

ASKING FOR MORE AND MORE

Everyone is hungry sometimes, but for many, hunger is an urgent problem. Some people do not have enough food to stay healthy, and others face starvation.

Food Security

Food security means having enough quality food to meet a person's **nutrition** needs. **Food insecurity**—not having the guarantee of enough good food—ranges from having poor-quality food, to occasionally being unable to afford food, to full-scale **famine**.

The world **population** is around 6.7 billion (2008), and is likely to rise to more than 9 billion by 2050. The growing population is a concern, but it is not the main problem.

World Economic Development

■ Developed economy   Not classified

■ Emerging economy   ■ Least developed economy

Earth Data

• The world population is growing at just over 1 percent, or 75 million people, a year.

• Nearly a billion people are going hungry around the world, and a billion more only have enough food some of the time. The number of people who lack food in sub-Saharan Africa has doubled since 1970.

• In India, 40 percent of children under five years of age are undernourished. Worldwide, 18,000 children die every day of hunger and hunger-related illness. A child dies every five seconds from **starvation** or illnesses brought about by **malnutrition** and poor-quality food.

The world's undeveloped nations suffer from the greatest poverty and hunger.

People who live in slums like this cannot afford good food.

We Have Enough

The world produces one and a half times as much food as we need. Yet about 800 million people do not have enough to eat, and another billion lack a reliable supply of good food. The number of people around the world going hungry is rising. Unfortunately, neither food supplies nor people are evenly distributed.

When people are very poor, they cannot afford food even if it is available. Even in rich countries, some people are poorer than others, and not everyone can afford good, nutritious food. Around one million people in the United States do not have the food they need.

Food prices can rise very quickly, moving good food out of the reach of more people. Over the coming years, feeding the world will become an increasingly difficult and urgent problem.

How Much Is Enough?

The United Nations (UN) considers 2,100 **calories** to be the daily level of food intake for an average person to stay healthy. Around one in seven people in the world do not have this amount of food regularly, leading to malnutrition and hunger. Many people are underfed on a daily basis for months or even years. It affects their mental and physical health and makes them vulnerable to illness.

Fat and Thin

While people in some areas starve, people elsewhere suffer from eating too much food. Famine causes starvation and malnutrition in areas such as sub-Saharan Africa, shantytowns in Indonesia, slums in Brazil, and isolated villages in the Andes and the Himalayas. Yet in parts of the **developed world**, eating too much is causing heart disease, **diabetes**, and other life-threatening conditions. Nearly two-thirds of the adult population of the United States is overweight, and half of those people are **obese** (grossly overweight.) Scotland has the second highest obesity rate in the world. Both too much food and too little puts people's health at risk.

The richest people in the United States or Scotland are not actually the fattest. Generally, poorer people are more likely to be obese than richer people because the low-quality processed foods that poor people can afford provide a bad diet. These people are often **malnourished** (even though they are large), as their food is not nutritious. Healthier foods—such as fresh fruit, vegetables, and lean meat—cost more, and many people just cannot afford them.

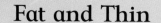

Obesity threatens the health of many people in developed countries.

Rising Prices

As food has become more expensive over recent years, the number of people unable to afford good food has risen around the world. According to the World Bank, for each rise of 1 percent in food prices, the calorie intake of the poorest people falls by 0.5 percent. In the United Kingdom, an average household spends only 10 percent of its income on food. However, the poorest people in the world need to spend 50 to 80 percent of their income on food. There is little room for them to spend more.

Demonstrators carry an over-sized model of a corn cob to protest against rules that will harm farmers in Mexico (2008).

Desperate people, faced with rising food prices and the threat of starvation, fight to get food. In 2007 and 2008, there were food riots in Morocco, Yemen, Mexico, Guinea, Mauritania, Senegal, and Uzbekistan. In April 2008, Haitian troops opened fire on people rioting about food prices, killing four of them. The price of beans, rice, and fruit had risen 50 percent in a year.

Trouble Ahead

There are more problems on the horizon: Although the world produces enough food now, this could quickly change. More land is being taken away from food production and put to other uses, such as building cities and roads, as well as growing nonfood crops. In addition, climate change is altering the patterns of what will grow in different places. All these factors may lead to **harvests** being reduced in the near future.

Planet Watch

» The United Nations set a goal to halve world hunger by 2015. It will take considerable political change to achieve this goal, and we are not on target at the moment.

» People in developed areas such as the United States, Europe, and Australia will have to change their eating patterns. The demands of wealthier nations for more food put too much strain on the world's food supply chain.

2

CAUSES BEHIND
A CRISIS

Rising oil prices, rising demand for land, and the early effects of climate change are all pushing up food prices around the world, causing a crisis for the world's hungry.

Oil and Food

Oil prices have climbed, driven partly by increasing demand. As the economies of China and India expand, these countries need more oil, and this puts pressure on supply. Conflict and political tension make the oil supply uncertain, and the price rises as people worry that supplies will be interrupted.

Rising oil prices push up other costs, including food prices, as oil is used in farming and food production. Farmers need fuel for their vehicles and machinery, and oil is used in making **fertilizers** and **agrochemicals**. Transporting and processing food costs more, too. As the price of food spirals upward, people in poverty are the first to suffer.

Wealthy people's demand for more meat drives up the prices for average shoppers like this woman.

Land for Other Uses

Expensive oil has led to increased use of biofuels to power vehicles. Biofuels are made from plant matter or animal waste, and some land is used to grow crops specifically for fuel. The increasing demand for biofuels will take even more land away from food production and push up food prices farther.

As the world population grows, people need somewhere to live. Land is taken from farming and developed as towns and cities with housing, schools, workplaces, roads, and factories.

> Farming cattle produces less food per acre than growing crops.

Meat and Milk

In countries such as China and India, more people are becoming rich (though many others still live on very little money). As people earn more, they want to spend their extra money on meat, fish, eggs, and dairy products. But this increased demand drives up prices.

An increasing amount of land is used to raise meat- and dairy-producing animals. It is used both as **pasture**—grassland for animals to graze—and as cropland to grow grain for animal feed. Animals are not very efficient in turning the plants they eat into meat, milk, or eggs, so land used for farming animals is less productive than **arable land**. At present, a third of the world's grain harvest is fed to **livestock**.

Staple Foods

For many people in the world, food consists mostly of basic **staples**, which they eat in large amounts. If they can afford it, they add extras, such as fruit, vegetables, meat, or spices, to make the food more nutritious and tasty.

Staples such as rice, wheat, corn, potatoes, sorghum, and cassava contain complex **carbohydrates** that give the body energy. Although people can survive without the extras for a while, they cannot do without staples for long. A poor harvest of wheat or rice can quickly lead to a famine.

Farmers in many places have stopped growing important crops of staple foods because they can only charge a low price for them. Instead, they grow **cash crops**—crops that are **exported** for a high price, such as coffee, cotton, or cocoa beans. The farmers are then vulnerable to world markets. If the outside world does not buy enough coffee or cotton, farmers are left with no money and with a crop that will not feed their families. Growing cash crops can lead to a shortage of affordable food for local people, including farmers themselves.

Vicious Circle

When farming families run out of food and money, they sometimes have to sell their farming tools to pay for food. They cannot return to farming later if conditions improve. Food production then drops further, the farming communities become even poorer, and the problem becomes rapidly worse.

Famine victims wait for food aid.

Who Will Gain and Lose from Rising Food Prices?

- Large losers
- Moderate losers
- Moderate gainers
- Large gainers
- No data

The people losing the most from rising food prices are in the world's poorest regions. People here cannot afford to pay the high prices for food. They also cannot grow enough to sell food for the high prices that would get them out of poverty.

Leaving the Land

In many parts of the world, people give up farming and move into towns and cities in the hope of a better, more prosperous life, leaving fewer people to farm the land and produce food. Countries then need to import more food, and they are very reliant on world food markets. It is not just a problem in developing countries; in the United Kingdom, the number of people working full time in farming dropped by nearly a third between 1986 and 1996.

As food shortages hit, the countries that produce food stop exporting it and keep it for their own consumption. Those that need to buy food have to pay more, if they can find it at all. Some countries have taken action to stem the outflow of food. Russia added a 40 percent export tax to wheat in January 2008, making the price so high that little wheat will be exported. Argentina is not allowing any more exporters to register to export wheat, and Vietnam suspended all rice exports at the end of 2007.

PLANET WATCH

» Forty percent of the dry land on Earth is used for agriculture. Of the rest, much cannot be used for farming because it is desert or mountains, is far from where people live, or has been built upon.

» An area the size of South America is used for growing food crops, and more land is used to keep and feed livestock. Ten billion animals are raised for food in the United States each year.

3 HOW THINGS GO WRONG

Problems such as crop disease, bad weather, and war can all lead to lost harvests and have disastrous results on the supply of food.

Crop Failure

Crops are living plants; they can be killed by disease, damage, or problems such as pests and molds. Diseases and pests can destroy a whole harvest, causing famine. This type of disaster has happened throughout history. For example, in 1845–52, a type of mold destroyed potatoes in Ireland, leading to a famine that killed 11.5 million people.

A swarm of locusts appears near Anakalang in Indonesia. They destroy crops by eating the leaves of plants.

Wars destroy farmland and crops, and take farmers away from the land.

Bad Weather

Crops can be destroyed by natural disasters such as floods, wildfires, and tropical storms, and some of the worst famines in history have been caused by bad weather. In 1969, a famine in China that killed 20 million people was caused by catastrophic floods. As the climate changes, **droughts** and floods will become more frequent in some areas.

In 2007, 57 countries in Africa, Asia, and Latin America were affected by severe flooding. At the same time, drought and heat reduced harvests in Asia, Europe, Sudan, Mozambique, and Uruguay. Drought caused the worst winter harvest in 10 years in 2007–08.

War and Political Problems

Wars have destroyed crops and caused famines for thousands of years. When farmers go to war, no one is left to tend the land. When farm workers are killed or injured, they cannot return to restore the land or continue farming after the war.

Sometimes, the need for farmland is the cause of war, as in the African nation of Darfur, where climate change has been the trigger. Drought has forced the Baggara nomads, who herd camels, to take their livestock farther south in search of water. They have moved onto farmland, and conflict has arisen with the farmers who were cultivating the land.

Looking for Farmland

Much of the usable land on Earth is farmed already, yet the need for farmland increases all the time. A way to tackle this is to claim more land for farming.

One way to gain land is to clear forest, as often happens in Southeast Asia or South America. In South America, rain forest is cleared to grow soybeans for export to China, for land to graze cattle and grow cattle food, and to grow corn for biofuels.

Slash and Burn

When people clear forest to use the land for farming, they often use the unsophisticated technique of "slash and burn." This means that they cut back the **vegetation**, fell the trees, then burn anything remaining to clear the forest floor.

The ground cleared by slash and burn techniques is productive for only a few years, as the soil quickly **erodes**, and nutrients are not renewed. Without the constant recycling of vegetation falling onto the ground and decaying, returning nutrients to the soil, nutrients are used up and not replenished.

Within five years, the farmers need to clear more forest, as they cannot get good harvests from the burned land. The search for new land to farm is damaging the world's ecosystem and endangering the delicate balance of the planet.

Careless Farming

Farmland that is not treated properly does not stay productive. Large areas of northern Africa have turned to desert because of both climate change and poor land use—where the land has been poorly managed, the soil has eroded.

Erosion occurs when the land is exposed and dried out by drought. The soil, which is usually held in place by the roots of plants and trees, dries to dust and is blown away by the wind. Once the topsoil has gone, plants cannot grow. The same problem occurred in the United States during the dustbowl years of 1930–36, when nearly 100 million acres (40 million ha) of farmland became useless.

In 1930s America, poor farming practices and dry weather led to the loss of millions of acres of farmland.

Expanses of bare land reveal the extent of deforestation around the Amazon.

Small Farmers Driven Out

In many parts of the world, small farms are quickly disappearing as large-scale farms take over. Large, industrial farmers have more political and economic power than small farmers. Often, they divert water from rivers to water their crops or take it from underground, meaning that there is no water supply left for smaller farms. The larger farms can afford to sell their produce more cheaply than small farms, too, quickly driving them out of business.

Fish Famine

Poor management affects other sources of food as well. Many areas of the sea are being overfished, and fish stocks are dropping to dangerously low levels as people demand more fish: Consumption rose sixfold between 1950 and 1997. In some places, quota laws limit the number of fish that boats may take in order to protect fish stocks. Yet large, industrialized fishing vessels can catch huge quantities of fish, and they may even dump dead fish back in the sea if they have gone over their quota.

In many areas, a combination of pollution running into the sea and warmer seas resulting from climate change are further damaging fish populations. Traditional, local fishermen are finding that the fish have died or are no longer visiting their usual areas, and there is nothing to catch.

PLANET WATCH

» From 2000 to 2005, 25.7 million acres (10.4 million ha) of rain forest were permanently deforested yearly. The land is used for soybeans, cattle, cash crops such as sugar and coffee, and building.

» In 2003, nearly a third of open-sea fisheries around the world were failing, producing less than 10 percent of their original quantities.

» The number of fish caught between 1994 and 2003 fell by 13 percent.

4 WASTE NOT, WANT NOT

Earth Data

- In the United States, agencies take spare food from restaurants and give it to the hungry.

- A "love food, hate waste" campaign started in the United Kingdom in 2007. In the program's first year, UK citizens saved £300 million ($440 million) worth of food.

People in wealthier countries have become wasteful. From individuals to whole nations, we have gotten used to throwing food away and eating more than we need.

Throwing Food Away

In cultures where food is scarce, people show respect to others by offering them food, and to reject or leave it is considered rude. Elsewhere, food has been plentiful for so long that the situation has reversed, and leaving food, or providing too much, is an acceptable sign of wealth. When people do leave food, they often throw it away—they no longer have the cooking skills or the inclination to make meals from leftovers, as previous generations have done.

Preparing more food than will be eaten is a common practice in wealthy societies.

Food waste often includes some that is perfectly edible.

Bigger Plates

Restaurants are often very wasteful of food. They make more food than they can sell, afraid of running out and upsetting customers. At the end of the day, the surplus is thrown away.

Offers of "all you can eat" are a common way of attracting customers, and portions are larger than they used to be. In the United States, restaurant portions have increased significantly since the 1970s. This makes customers think they are getting good value for their money, but inevitably much of the food is wasted. There is always more food, and it appears to have lost its value.

Mountains of Waste

Supermarkets often stock more food than they can sell, and then if the food passes its expiration date, the shops throw it away unsold. People pressed for time shop once a week, buying large quantities without planning their meals. Much of the food

goes to waste. If it is not eaten before it goes bad, or passes its expiration date, people throw it away, afraid it will make them sick if they eat it. Around a third of the food bought from supermarkets in the United Kingdom is thrown away.

In developed societies, people have become used to buying food that looks perfect and is uniform in shape and size. This is not only because consumers want their food to look nice. When food producers use mechanized processes to pick and pack food, the machinery often cannot deal with different sizes and shapes. Fruits and vegetables that are odd shapes or sizes may be sent for making processed foods, but they are often simply thrown away.

All this amounts to a vast mountain of food that is bought, sometimes cooked, sometimes served, and then thrown away. The cost of food thrown away in the United States was estimated at $43 billion a year in 2004.

Pansrithong Guava
ฝรั่งแป้นสีทอง
39 /kg

Vietnam | Salee
Dragonfruit Guava
แก้วมังกรเวียดนาม ฝรั่งสาลี
59 /kg 24 /kg

Fragrant Pear
สาลี่หอม
65 /kg

Eating fresh fruit is healthy, but not everyone can afford it.

Too Little and Too Much

While **subsistence farming** in parts of Africa, India, and Asia produces barely enough for people to live on, industrialized farming in Europe and the United States produces more food than farmers can sell. The European Union (EU) has had surplus stocks of food for many years. Until recently, the U.S. Department of Agriculture bought up stocks of cheese, corn, and other foods and stored them in warehouses and even caves.

These stores of unneeded food are commonly known as a "butter mountain," "milk lake," and so on. The EU and the U.S. Department of Agriculture buy surplus crops from farmers at a guaranteed price to keep prices high enough for the farmers to make a living. If prices were able to find their own level, the large amounts of food available would cause prices to fall, and it would be unprofitable for farmers to produce it.

The food in the food mountains is eventually either destroyed or sold to poorer countries for low prices. Traditionally, food from the EU and U.S. food mountains has been dumped in Africa, but this depresses the prices local farmers can charge for their produce.

Set-Aside Land

The EU has even paid farmers to set land aside—not to farm it—to prevent surplus production. Set-aside land could easily be pulled back into use for food production if it was necessary.

Ideally, set-aside land would grow food for hungry people, but it was a challenge to make this work. Wages and other production costs are high in developed countries, so the food produced on set-aside land was too expensive for undeveloped countries to buy without **subsidies** or aid. The EU suspended the set-aside policy in 2008.

Corn, Cattle, and Cars

In the "corn belt"—the area centered on the corn-producing state of Iowa—more corn has always been produced than is needed. Policy in the United States has discouraged exporting corn, and this has led to corn being used as animal feed. Limiting corn exports keeps international prices high and guarantees a better price for the corn that is exported. Political actions to protect farmers have unforeseen consequences for hungry people in many parts of the world.

In some places, corn is now used to make biofuels, reducing a country's dependence on oil and oil-producing countries. Using food to make fuel may mean higher food prices, and it may look to hungry people as if food is being wasted.

PLANET WATCH

» At the start of 2007, the EU was storing 13 million tons (12 million t) of grain, 1.1 million (1 million t) of sugar, and 265 million bottles of wine.

» In 2007, the stock of grain kept by the United Nations fell to 54 days' worth, the lowest it has been in 26 years. This would not go far if a major disaster occurred.

» In 2007, the world produced 24 million tons (22 million t) less grain than we actually consumed. Further years of underproduction will rapidly eat into the UN's store.

European farmers used to be paid to leave land fallow, or not farmed.

5

A CHANGING CLIMATE

As the climate changes, some crops will no longer grow where they have traditionally been farmed, and some farmland will be lost completely.

Why Is the Climate Changing?

Over the last hundred years (1906–2005), the world has been getting warmer, with the average temperature rising by nearly 1.3°F (0.74°C). Most scientists agree that the rise is caused by increased levels of carbon gases in the **atmosphere**. These gases, particularly carbon dioxide and methane, trap heat near the Earth, making the planet warmer. As the concentration of the gases increases, the temperature of the air, ground, and seas rises.

Severe drought in northern Tanzania, East Africa, has destroyed this crop of corn.

Flooding destroys the rice in paddy fields.

Human activity that involves burning fossil fuels such as coal, oil, and gas adds extra carbon gases to the atmosphere. The gases have been building up for the last 200 years, since the start of the Industrial Revolution.

When we burn fossil fuels, carbon locked away in the fuel combines with oxygen in the atmosphere to make carbon dioxide. Carbon stored over millions of years is released all at once. The level of carbon gases in the atmosphere now is higher than it has ever been in the last 800,000 years.

Changing Weather Patterns

As the temperature of Earth warms up, the climate changes in many ways, and not just that everywhere gets a little warmer. The weather system is a delicate balance that involves rain patterns, wind systems, and sea currents. The warming climate is already producing more droughts, floods, and storms.

As the air and seas warm up, the ice near the North and South poles melts and the water from the melting ice runs into the sea, slowly raising the level of the seas all over the world. Low-lying land floods more easily, and eventually some areas will be completely flooded.

A lot of farmland around fertile river **deltas** is at increased risk of flooding. Frequent flooding by seawater brings too much salt into the soil, making it difficult to grow crops on the land even after the floods have receded.

Farming and the Weather

Changing weather patterns will affect food and farming in many ways. Some areas may become too hot and dry—or too wet—to grow anything at all. At the same time, some areas that currently cannot be farmed may become warm enough to farm.

The pattern of the seasons is changing, too, with spring coming earlier in many places and summer lasting longer. Summers may be drier and winters wetter.

Changing Farms

Changing temperatures and rainfall patterns mean that some crops will no longer grow in areas where they grew traditionally. Farmers will need to adapt, perhaps changing the crops they grow and the methods they use.

Livestock farmers will be affected, too. If grassland dies out in warmer, drier conditions, farmers will no longer be able to keep cattle on their land. They may need to turn to hardier animals, such as goats, which can tolerate harsh conditions and eat scrub. But these animals do not produce as large yields as cattle, so a drop in production would be the result.

Pests on the Move

Just as plants are adapted to particular climate patterns, so are the diseases and pests that affect them. Warmer weather over a wider band of land will extend the range of pests and diseases that attack crops. Farmers will have to tackle unfamiliar insects and diseases that move into their area as the weather changes.

Warmer winters and earlier springs will make it easier for pests to survive, and longer summers will mean that some insect pests can produce more generations. In Scotland, some types of **aphid** produce 18 generations each summer, but this could rise to 23 generations by the year 2050.

For thousands of years, locusts have plagued hot areas of Africa, the Middle East, Australia, and parts of Asia. Usually, locusts are solitary, but weather patterns can lead them to breed quickly and swarm. Swarms of locusts strip all the vegetation over huge areas, devastating crops. More areas will be affected by locusts as weather patterns change.

Upsala Glacier, Los Glaciares National Park, Argentina. Photo taken in 1928.

This glacier in Argentina has melted away, so the fresh water it once stored as ice is no longer available.

Upsala Glacier, Los Glaciares National Park, Argentina. Photo taken in 2004.

26

This rice field in Thailand has been completely parched by drought.

PLANET WATCH

» Glaciers are melting faster than at any time in the last 5,000 years.

» The Tibetan plateau has 46,298 glaciers, covering more than 60,000 sqare miles (155,000 sq km). They will reduce by 50 percent every 10 years.

» From 1980 to 1999, glaciers shrank an average of 11.8 inches (30 cm) a year; in 2006, the average was 5 feet (1.5 m).

» Glaciers in the Himalayas provide water for 40 percent of the world's population.

Water Shortage

Drier summers will increase the need for irrigation, or watering, of crops. Irrigated land can produce up to four times as much food as unirrigated land, yet many areas are currently unirrigated. They may produce just enough for the needs of farmers now, but if rainfall decreases, additional water will be essential.

In many places, freshwater for farming comes from glaciers, or frozen mountain rivers. In summer, parts of the glaciers melt and the water from them runs in rivers through the farmed lowlands, providing water for crops. In winter, the glacier freezes again. Climate change is disrupting this pattern, and from South America to Asia, glaciers are melting and not refreezing.

Farmland in India and China is irrigated from rivers such as the Ganges, the Yangtze, and the Yellow River. The water comes from glaciers in the Himalayas that could be gone by 2035, cutting the flow of rivers by up to 70 percent. India and China produce more than half the world's rice harvest and are the top producers of wheat, too. These crops need the glacier-melted waters.

Towns First

When water is in short supply, small-scale farmers are the first to lose. Water is diverted from rivers or pumped from underground to feed large farms and towns. This hits small farmers again, since their wells run dry and rivers are depleted.

When water is diverted from small farms like this one in Zambia to supply towns, farmers and food supply suffer.

Adapting Crops

Where one crop will no longer grow, farmers may need to grow a different crop. They might choose a **strain** of wheat that is more resistant to drought, for example. Sometimes, farmers may need to give up one crop entirely and grow a different one. Areas of Canada currently used to grow fruit and maple trees will have a climate more suitable for farming wheat by 2050. Many farmers will need financial help and education to change the types of crops they grow.

New Methods

Some new farming methods will help farmers produce crops as the weather patterns change. For instance, agroforestry involves growing crops or keeping livestock between trees. The trees help to keep the topsoil in place and may also provide a crop, such as apples or coconuts.

Drip irrigation can help farmers deal with the changing climate, as it provides a very slow trickle of water directly to plants. This makes more efficient use of water than spraying.

The Water Cycle

The amount of water present on Earth is stable, but the water is constantly recycled as it evaporates from land and sea and falls again as rain. Some is used by plants, animals, and people, but all is eventually released again to flow into rivers and the sea or evaporate into the air. At any one time, less than three percent of the water on Earth is fresh, and the rest is in the oceans and seas. Only freshwater can be used to water crops, but most of the freshwater is locked up in polar ice and glaciers. If ice melts and is not replenished, the amount of freshwater will drop further.

Seawater is salty, and it cannot be used for drinking or watering crops unless the salt is removed. Desalination plants heat the salt water, creating salt and steam. The steam is then **condensed** back to a liquid that is safe to drink. Some desalination plants use solar or hydroelectric power, which do not produce the carbon gases that cause climate change.

PLANET WATCH

» A small-scale project started in Ladakh, India, makes an artificial glacier. Water is diverted from a stream to run through a shady area where it freezes in winter. The glacier melts in summer, providing water for drinking and irrigation.

» An artificial tree developed in Spain traps water from the air at night and releases it in the day, cooling the surrounding air. With enough artificial trees, rain would eventually fall.

The desalination plant draws water from the nearby sea and removes the salt. The resulting water is safe to drink.

6

SCIENCE TO THE RESCUE?

In the past, the world fought a looming food crisis with new scientific methods of farming. Can we do it again?

The "Green Revolution"

After World War II, the population grew very quickly, rising from 2.5 billion in 1950 to 5 billion in 1987. Many people feared a catastrophic food shortage and widespread famine, but science rose to the challenge with the "Green Revolution." New strains of crops, new farming methods, and new chemicals to increase yields were developed in a few years, averting disaster. Agriculture became a big business venture, closely tied to science and dominated by huge international corporations. These businesses changed the face of food production forever—in both good and bad ways.

Earth Data

- From 2007 to 2012, fertilizer use will increase 1.7 percent a year. Nearly 70 percent of the extra fertilizer will be used in Asia.

- In 2007 and 2008, the world used more than 220 tons (200 million t) of fertilizer.

Spraying crops with pesticides helps to protect them, but it may leave toxic residues in foods.

Modern science can help develop plants that will be resilient, provide extra nutrition, and produce good yields.

Many people believe a new Green Revolution is needed to confront a new set of problems in food supply. While politics must tackle the problem of distributing the food that is grown, science can help to increase yields and provide crops that can cope with climate change. A combination of old and new methods will be needed, refining again some of the developments of the twentieth century and exploring completely new avenues.

Chemical Cocktails

Diseases and animal pests destroy around a third of unprotected crops in some locations. Food shortages could be eased considerably by saving crops that are lost to pests.

Farmers have used chemicals to fight disease and pests for many years, but there are problems with pesticides. Overuse of the dangerous chemical DDT to protect crops damaged both wildlife and people years ago. Some chemicals are becoming less effective as pests and diseases change to become resistant to them. And many people worry about the levels of chemicals that are present in food, or washed into rivers by rain that has fallen onto sprayed crops. While chemicals have a part to play in farming, they are no longer a cure-all.

Better Breeding

For thousands of years, farmers have chosen the best plants and animals from which to breed new generations. They found by trial and error that they could breed cows that produced more milk, or wheat plants that produced more grain. This process is called **selective breeding**.

During the 1960s, scientists bred new types of grain that produced a high yield. This helped the world to cope with the threatened food crisis caused by the rising population. Scientists now also breed selectively for resistance to disease and pests. By breeding stronger strains, we can reduce our dependence on pesticides and other chemicals.

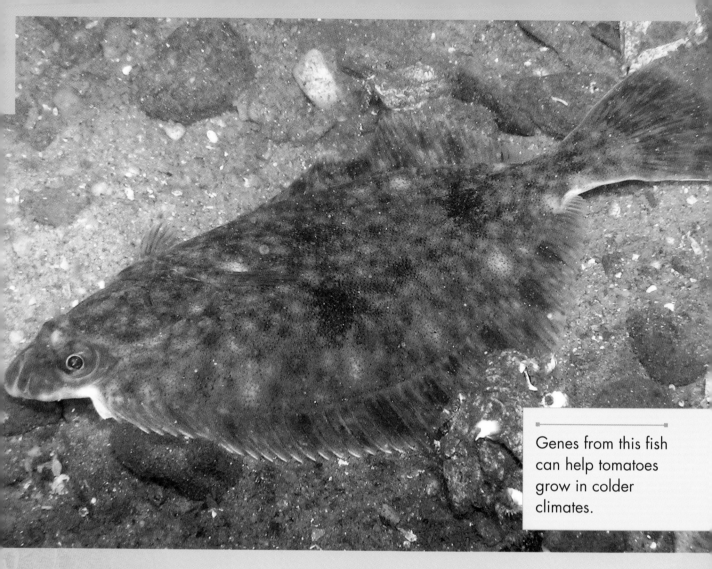

Genes from this fish can help tomatoes grow in colder climates.

Using Genes

Selective breeding is a slow process, as the farmer has to wait for the new generation to grow before breeding from it, but scientists can now change plants and animals much more quickly. Using **genetic engineering**, they can make changes directly to the **genes** of a plant or animal.

Genetic engineering works by taking a small amount of **DNA** (the material that carries genetic information) from one plant or animal and adding it to the DNA of another. The DNA chosen carries the instructions for a characteristic that scientists want to copy. A plant or animal that has been changed in this way is **genetically modified** (GM).

Characteristics can be copied between plants and animals that would not normally interbreed. For example, a gene from a fish that lives in a very cold sea can be put into tomatoes to make them frost-resistant.

What Can GM Do?

Plants can be genetically modified to give them resistance to pests and diseases, enabling them to grow in different conditions, such as drier, wetter, hotter, or colder areas. So far, GM crops have not given a higher yield than ordinary crops. GM food crops grown in the United States and Argentina have shown no increase in yield at all. In fact, yield from GM soybeans in the United States was 10 percent less than for similar non-GM strains grown in exactly the same conditions.

Scientists do not agree about how GM crops can best help to solve the food crisis. It may be through producing more resilient plants.

Nearly one-quarter of the calories consumed in the world come from rice, so it is a very important staple. Traditional rice plants cannot cope with floods, but climate change will bring more flooding to rice-growing areas. Some genetically modified rice can withstand flooding and even saltwater. Another type of GM rice produces a lot of grain but has a short, thick stem so that it does not fall over in bad weather. Both of these could help farmers to maintain yields in a changing climate.

Added Nutrition

GM foods may combat malnutrition by providing foods with modified nutritional value. "Golden rice" provides extra vitamin A and may help to prevent some of the 500,000 cases of blindness every year that result from lack of vitamin A. Researchers in the United States have produced a carrot with extra calcium (a mineral needed for growing bones and teeth). These crops would help to keep people healthy, providing more of the vitamins and minerals they need.

PLANET WATCH

» 140,000 varieties of rice have been developed by selective breeding without using GM techniques.

» Thailand and Vietnam, which account for half of all rice exports, have banned GM rice. The ban followed the accidental release of a type of GM rice into the food supply chain by a U.S. producer. The rice had not been approved for human consumption. The EU and Japan banned imports of American rice as a result.

» Most of the GM crops in the world (98 percent) are farmed by the United States, Canada, Argentina, China, and Brazil.

Farmers prepare fields where a previous crop had been destroyed by floods. Flood-resistant rice might help farmers in the future.

GM Animals

GM techniques can be used to modify animals, too. Researchers developed a cow that cannot get BSE or "mad cow" disease, a disease that can be passed to people who eat meat from infected cattle. Other scientists have produced cows and sheep that give milk with extra protein.

Problems with GM

Some people worry that GM crops may bring health risks that will emerge in the future, or may contaminate natural plants. Another criticism is that GM crops have been developed to make money and are are too expensive for farmers in developing countries.

Some GM crops have been developed to resist a powerful weed killer. Farmers can spray the crops with this single weed killer to get rid of all weeds, but they must buy this particular weed killer, no matter what its price. Poor farmers cannot always afford it, so they cannot benefit.

Other GM crops produce "suicide seeds" that will not grow into plants. Farmers cannot harvest seed for the following year, but must pay for more seed. Although the producers who developed the crops need to make money, the cost is too high for farmers in poor countries.

Protestors destroy a field of genetically modified corn in Mauvezin, France, 2001.

We may need to learn to eat foods that are unfamiliar to us.

Beef without Cows

If everyone gave up eating meat and dairy products, the farmland available for crops would double, but that is not likely to happen. An alternative is to produce meat by growing muscle tissue in a laboratory. Scientists are working to develop products such as minced beef or chicken nuggets, all grown from a few cells taken from a single, unharmed animal. Lab-grown meat would not contain any traces of the chemicals and medicines that are often fed to farm animals and would not pollute the land with large amounts of animal waste.

New Foods

New foods could help us to feed the world. Quorn is a meat substitute made from a fungus (like a mold) called mycoprotein. It is grown in large towers 130 feet (40 m) tall, feeding on sugar syrup and doubling in mass every five hours. Just 2.5 square miles (4 sq km) of land filled with towers growing mycoprotein could provide enough to feed a billion people.

PLANET WATCH

» A new method of rice production, the system of rice intensification (SRI), adapts conventional farming methods to use 40 percent less water and no chemical fertilizers, yet produces 30 percent higher yields. Using SRI, India could meet its grain target of 242 million tons (220 million t) by 2012.

» A competition launched in 2008 offers a prize of $1 million to the first producer of a commercial-standard "chicken" ready-meal made from artificially grown meat.

7

WORKING FOR A FAIRER WORLD

Science may help us to solve the problem of world hunger, but politics has an important role to play and could provide solutions to the current crisis more quickly.

Food Out of Reach

One-seventh of the world does not have enough to eat, yet many of the world's hungry are in countries that have food surpluses. India, for example, produces more food than it needs, and yet it has many hungry people. More than 90 percent of the world's hungry cannot afford food, even though it may be available to buy. Getting food to people who need it is the quickest way to solve the problem, but this is a political issue as much as a problem of geography or transportation. Many people believe that world hunger will not be solved until world poverty is solved: People must own the land they need to grow food, or have the money to buy food.

Governments and aid groups bring food to hungry people, but this is just a short-term solution.

36

Local and International Help

In some countries, governments subsidize food for the poor, or guarantee that people will receive a basic ration of food. In Cuba, from 1959 to 1989, all people were guaranteed enough good food to provide 1,900 calories a day. In India, the government buys rice from farmers and distributes it around the country in fair-price shops. The country's poorest people—about a third of the population—can apply for a ration card that entitles them to 22 pounds (10 kg) of rice a month at a price they can afford.

Charitable gifts of food to regions hit by famine or natural disaster can help hungry people in the short term. But international aid in the form of cheap or free food is not a long-term solution to world hunger. Many experts point out that sending free or cheap food into an area undermines local farmers, making it uneconomic for them to produce food for sale locally. Aid needs to concentrate on enabling people to be self-sufficient and develop their own farming skills and resources. Most charitable work in areas of food insecurity follows this aim.

The UN WFP

The World Food Programme (WFP) was set up by the UN in 1963 to combat food insecurity. The WFP sends food aid in times of crisis, such as natural disasters, wars, and failed harvests. It works to improve the nutrition of vulnerable people and helps people to provide their own food so that they will not depend on aid in the future. The WFP is charged with meeting the UN's goal to halve world hunger by 2015.

The WFP teaches people how to grow their own food rather than wait for it to be given to them. These banana plants provide food for the community. They also provide income for the farmer.

Fair Trade

Farmers can only make enough to live on without aid if they can sell their crops for a fair, sustainable price. Supermarkets in richer countries have driven down the price that farmers around the world are paid for the food they produce, pushing many into poverty. The fair trade movement grew up to pay people a fair amount for the food they produce. Many people will pay for fair trade food as they know farmers will benefit.

Critics of fair trade say that it distorts natural price competition and that it encourages farmers to grow crops for export (for high prices) rather than for local people to buy (at lower prices).

What Can You Do?

There are simple measures that we can all take, beginning with avoiding waste. Wasting less will help to keep food prices down, helping people who cannot afford rising costs.

Tilapia, a type of fish, represents the most efficient conversion of feed into animal protein.

Members of a Karen hill tribe family prepare food for a traditional meal in Chang Mai, Thailand.

We can make careful choices about food, too. By eating less meat and dairy products, we can ease the burden on the world's grain supplies. If everyone eats a little less, eventually the change in demand will lead to lower production.

We can also buy meat and fish that take less energy to produce. Tilapia is a type of fish that is farmed all over the world, and effectively converts feed into animal protein. It takes only 3.7 pounds (1.7 kg) of feed to reproduce 2.2 pounds (1 kg) of fish.

Buying local produce helps to keep local farmers in business and reduces the impact that transporting food long distances has on the climate. Buying food from far away is not only bad for the climate, but it also encourages farmers to grow crops for export and not for the local community.

The Bigger Picture

Feeding the world's growing population is an urgent problem that can only be solved by an international effort. The complex interplay of climate change, politics, and poverty demands a solution that draws on science and governments. Most of all, the problem demands that people care enough to help those who are in need of food.

PLANET WATCH

» In March 2008, the WFP announced that, due to the rising price of rice, it would have to cut its food aid program unless donations increased.

» The WFP receives around $3 billion a year from national governments, corporations, and private donors.

» Farmers and warehouse owners in some parts of the world mount armed guards over their rice stocks to prevent looters and raiders from stealing it.

FACTS AND FIGURES

World Population Figures and Projections

Year	Population	Year	Population
1950	2.5 billion	2000	6 billion
1960	3 billion	2010	6.8 billion
1970	3.7 billion	2020	7.5 billion
1980	4.5 billion	2030	8.2 billion
1990	5.3 billion	2040	8.8 billion
		2050	9.3 billion

The table shows that the population of the world is growing at an enormous rate. In 100 years, the population of Earth will almost quadruple. Food production is not growing to match the rise in population.

- The people in the African country of Eritrea suffer from severe food insecurity. In 1995, one-third of the food the people ate was in the form of aid from other countries. By 2003, that amount increased to almost one-half.

- Based on the most current statistics, the country with the greatest proportion of underweight children is Afghanistan. The country with the greatest proportion of overweight children is Russia.

- Researchers expect wheat production in Africa to fall by up to 18 percent by 2030 as a result of climate change. The hardest hit nations will be Tanzania, Mozambique, and the Democratic Republic of the Congo, which will face increasing food insecurity.

Where Are the Undernourished People?

Notice that most of the undernourished areas are poor countries where farming and ranching are not well developed.

% of population undernourished

35% and more   20–34%   5–19%   2.5–4%   less than 2.5%   No data

How Much Food Energy Does a Person Get Each Day?

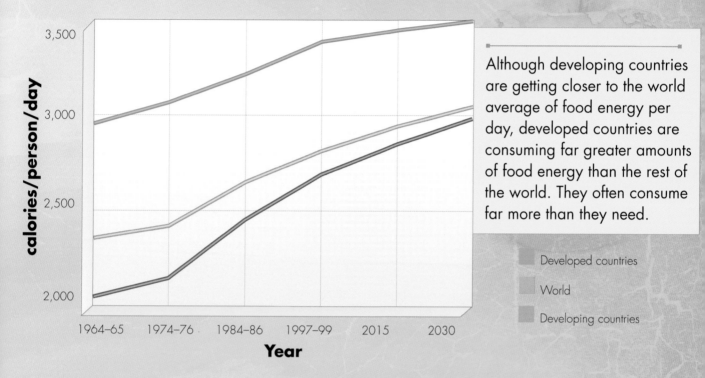

Although developing countries are getting closer to the world average of food energy per day, developed countries are consuming far greater amounts of food energy than the rest of the world. They often consume far more than they need.

Developed countries

World

Developing countries

How Much Land Could Be Used to Grow Food?

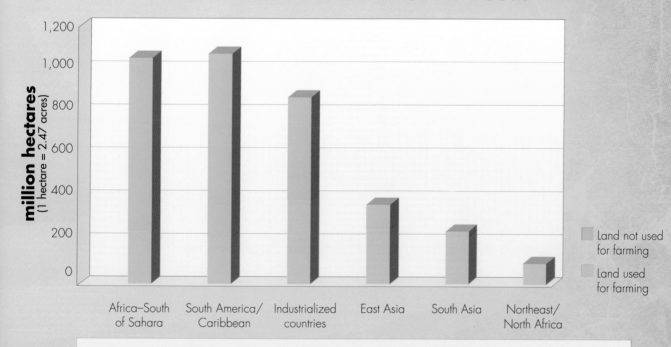

Land not used for farming

Land used for farming

Countries in Africa south of the Sahara and in South America have a great deal of land that could be farmed, but is not. The land either lies fallow or is used for other purposes. Other countries, such as those in southern Asia and northern Africa, have less land available for farming.

Glossary

agrochemicals
chemicals used in agriculture, such as fertilizers and pesticides

aphid
small insect that feeds on the sap of plants, damaging crops

arable land
land used to grow crops

atmosphere
the whole mass of air surrounding the Earth

biofuel
fuel made from biological material

calorie
a unit for measuring energy from food

carbohydrate
a complex chemical compound made of carbon, hydrogen, and oxygen that is an important source of energy from food

cash crop
a crop that is farmed to sell rather than to eat

condense
to make liquid from a gas by cooling it

delta
an area where a river spreads out in a triangular pattern of small channels as it joins the sea

developed world
countries with an advanced economy in which service industries and intelligence-based industries dominate

diabetes
a medical condition in which the body cannot properly control the level of sugar in the blood

DNA
genetic material made of complex protein chains; it carries the "instructions" to make a living being

drought
a period of extreme dryness, with no rain

erode
to wear away

export
to sell goods to another country

famine
an extreme shortage of food

fertilizer
chemicals added to the soil or fed to plants to encourage growth by providing nutrients

food insecurity
state of lacking a reliable source of sufficient, nutritious food

food security
state of having a reliable source of sufficient, nutritious food

gene
a sequence of DNA that carries the coding for a characteristic that is inherited

genetic engineering
a technique for working directly with genes to adapt the features of plants and animals

genetically modified
to change using genetic engineering techniques

harvest
crops that have been gathered at the end of the growing season

livestock
animals reared for food or profit, particularly farm animals

malnourished
state of having lacked nutrients and developed medical conditions as a result

malnutrition
when a person's diet contains insufficient nutrients, including protein, vitamins, and minerals

nutrition
the process of taking in and benefiting from food

obese
to be very overweight

pasture
the land used for grazing animals

population
the total number of people living in an area

protein
a complex chemical that is the building block of plant and animal tissue

rationing
limiting the amount each person can have

selective breeding
choosing plants or animals from which to breed in order to strengthen a particular feature

staple
basic foodstuff that supplies most of a person's needs

strain
a genetic variety of a plant or animal

starvation
the state of being starved, without nourishment

subsistence farming
farming that produces just enough for someone to live on

subsidies
extra money to help buy or produce something

vegetation
plants and trees

FURTHER READING

- *Chew on This* by Eric Schlosser and Charles Wilson (Houghton Mifflin, 2006)
- *A Kids' Guide to Hunger and Homelessness: How to Take Action* by Cathryn Berger Kaye (Free Spirit Publishing, 2007)
- *Poverty* (What if We Do Nothing) by Cath Senker (World Almanac Library, 2007)
- *Water Supply* (What if We Do Nothing) by Rob Bowden (Franklin Watts, 2006)
- *World Hunger* (21st Century Issues) by Steven Maddocks (World Almanac Library, 2005)

INDEX

WEB FINDER

www.30hourfamine.org/
An organization that gets youth involved in raising funds and awareness for world poverty.

www.farmafrica.org.uk/index.cfm
Group that provides training to people in eastern Africa to use better farming and ranching techniques that may end famine and poverty in the region.

www.cartercenter.org/health/agriculture/index.html
Former U.S. president Jimmy Carter's organization partners with groups that support farming and food production in underdeveloped countries.

www.wfp.org/country_brief/hunger_map/map/hungermap_popup/map_popup.html
Interactive map showing areas of the world and how many people are hungry there.

www.globalissues.org/TradeRelated/Poverty.asp
An explanation of the causes of poverty that contribute to food insecurity.

www.thehungersite.com
Click to donate food aid—it costs you nothing.